AF367999

Sales and operations planning
S&OP
in 14 steps

Cristina Peña Andrés

In collaboration with:

www.logisnet.com

*To those who make me feel happy and cheerful
every day with just their smile.*

*To Diego, Álvaro and Jorge, my greatest
treasure and legacy.*

Acknowledgements

This executive guide represents a project that has allowed me to fully develop a comprehensive overview of the supply chain, especially in terms of overall planning and project management.

I am indebted to Alberto Tundidor Díaz for his exhaustive work in reviewing the book and drafting the diagrams that accompany the text along with his contributions addressing the management of S&OP in SME's as well as all the cooperation and support he provided me to get it done on time.

I thank Mike Pagendam, Vice Executive President in Alimak Group and Head of Aftersales Business Area, for this opportunity to be in his team through this new position as I can continue creating value for Alimak facing a big challenge in my professional career.

Index

The author 11
Presentation 13
Introduction 17

1 What is the sales and operations
  planning process? 21

2 Where is S&OP used? 25

3 Who leads the planning process? 29

4 S&OP objectives 33

5 How to develop S&OP 39

6 S&OP meetings 43

7 The minutes of the meetings 49

8 S&OP frequency 53

9 Macro data applied to S&OP 57

10 The benefits of S&OP 61

11 S&OP as a process. 75

12 Identification of bottlenecks 81

13 General budgets. 85

14 Forecasts and plans. 89

Case study 1. 95
Case study 2. 99
Case study 3. 103
Case study 4. 107
Case study 5. 111

The author

 **Cristina Peña Andrés** (Madrid, 1977), holds a degree and master in industrial engineering from the Universidad Politécnica de Madrid. She has an International MBA from the Universidad del Escorial (Real Centro Universitario Escorial – Maria Cristina) and several university courses and diplomas related to foreign trade and business management.

She has been the senior director in a position related to foreign trade and logistics and international transport in a multinational construction company that exports to all five continents. She has been Group Parts Manager for Alimak Group, the worldwide leader in vertical access solutions, since November 2017.

At the same time she is professor at Fundación ICIL, a benchmark in logistics training. She has given numerous courses to professionals, lectured in seminars and contributed to trade journals.

She is co-author of the book *Crédito documentario. Guía para el éxito en su gestión* (Documentary Credit, a guide to its successful management) edited by Marge

Books in 2015. This first edition was followed by a second one in the same year, where a fully developed case study was included.

She is author of the book *Manual de transporte para el comercio internacional* (Transport manual for international trade), as well as its annex concerning the new amendments to the SOLAS Convention. She is also the author of the books *Negociación para el comercio internacional* (Negotiation for International Trade) and *Cómo participar en ferias comerciales* (How to Participate in Trade Shows).

 @cristinapenaand

 www.cristinapenaandres.com

For five years, I was Global Planning Manager (or S&OP Manager) in a multinational with sales offices all over the world to which the product is exported from a single manufacturing centre located in Spain.

The implementation of S&OP as a strategic process to align the highest level goals of the company with the day to day operations was a challenge I faced from the first day of assuming my responsibility.

Years later, I am proud of the result of that complex project. I see how this formal process flows, in an organized way, throughout the different levels of the company, impregnating itself in company culture like an intangible ingredient that characterizes its modus operandi nowadays.

In its infancy, it required a lot of discipline in creating routines, reports, master tables, analysis and, of course, meetings. I requested the cooperation of all areas in the company and had to reconcile many conflicting interests by means of diplomacy and intercultural negotiation.

I always portrayed the utmost seriousness and professionalism. However, I have no doubt that the definitive thrust I had in the project was the complete support of the organization's CEO, Tony Combe, whom I thank for entrusting me with that responsibility.

Now, after the experience, I am compiling in this manual the benefits of this process and its transcendence in aligning an entire organization in the achievement of goals – rolling out the high level ones downstream but mainly presenting a single truth for the management of the company.

Sales and operations planning

S&OP

in 14 steps

The sales and operations planning process, also known as S&OP, is the tool that helps to reconcile the planning, finances, sales and operations of a company, aligning all the goals of its different areas.

For there to be a consensus in the organization on the allocation of resources and the establishment of priorities, there must be absolute support from the top executive management of the company.

S&OP allows us to understand the market, i.e. its potential demand, complexity, trends and the company's share of it.

It also allows for internal analysis regarding the processes, capacities, available resources, attainable opportunities and current restrictions.

The key to the process is the interdepartmental and divisional communication system, both cross-ways as well as up and downstream. Regardless of the level of detail used in each case, the same information should always be distributed to everyone and it should be unique and transparent.

Based on this information, the company takes its strategic and operational decisions and all the members

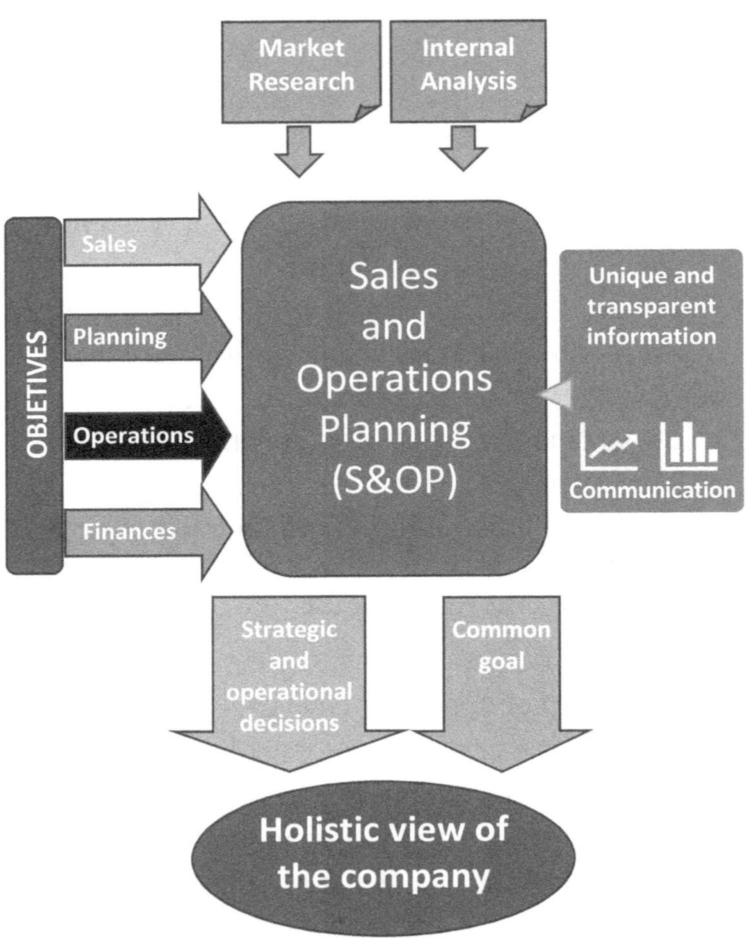

Market Research
Internal Analysis
OBJETIVES
Sales
Planning
Operations
Finances
Sales and Operations Planning (S&OP)
Unique and transparent information
Communication
Strategic and operational decisions
Common goal
Holistic view of the company

of the organization, in their respective fields of activity, can act proactively to face the necessary changes in the established time frame.

This operational methodology allows for there to be a holistic view of the company and for this to be shared by all the people who comprise it so they can direct their efforts in the same direction.

Example

In companies that do not have a sales and operations planning process in place, it is common to find that their strategic dynamics is based on a sales plan generated by their management without sharing information with the operational areas.

Only once completed is this sales plan distributed to all areas of the company as a mandate that must be fulfilled without taking into account its reality, i.e. without considering possible restrictions or even the total impossibility of achieving the required results.

Failure to meet the sales plan can lead to a hole in the company's profit and loss account when the results achieved do not match the income forecast.

On the other hand, low yields and negative turnover situations can also occur precisely by meeting a sales plan that was designed without taking possible production overcapacity into account.

1

What is the sales and operations planning process?

It is the formal process that aims to regularly analyze demand and supply and coordinates the sales, operations and finance areas thus allowing the company to have a structured review of its workload.

S&OP is one of the company's strategic processes and is usually integrated in the company's business plan insofar as it aims to balance the supply plan (purchases/production) and reconcile it with the sales plan.

Its ultimate purpose is to prevent excessive misalignment between supply and sales plans from producing one of two situations:

a) The company produces much more than it sells:

- Stockpiles increase, forcing a search for additional warehousing.
- The stock volume is, furthermore, an asset that puts the company's liquidity at risk.
- This situation represents an opportunity cost.

b) The company sells much more than it produces:

- Not all orders are supplied on time, with the consequent dissatisfaction of customers and possible erosion of business relationships.
- Penalties or additional costs associated with a charge for substandard service may be incurred.

Usually, the company cannot produce at a perfectly synchronized rhythm with demand since the inevitable fluctuations of this would result in an unbalanced production with possible episodes of high work load peaks followed by moments of minimal activity.

This production model would have a very high cost since it requires having infrastructure and resources available that could not always be exploited cost-effectively and leads to very irregular behaviour towards suppliers.

However, producing in a more stable way generates productivity gains, since the company's resources and, consequently, supply chain are optimized.

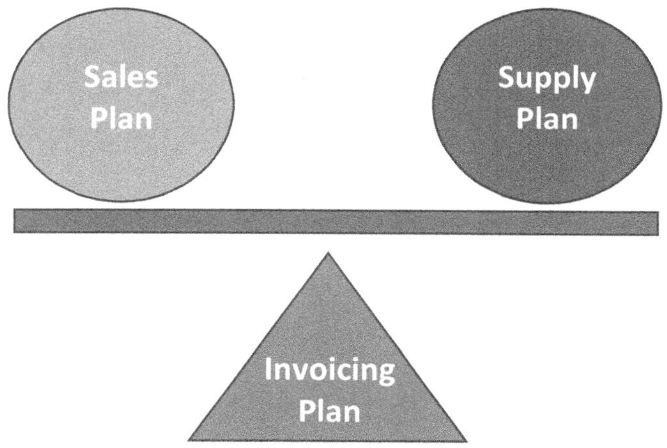

Sales
Plan
Supply
Plan
Invoicing
Plan

S&OP always seeks a progressive adaptation of production to demand trends which easier to manage and more profitable than following its volatility step by step.

In this sense, S&OP methodology is similar to the lean (manufacturing) philosophy.

The constant communication between the areas of the organization involved in S&OP contributes to achieving balance in the company's overall activity and to finding the most favourable situation for each area involved.

A coordinated sales and supply plan in close harmony with the invoicing plan is a result of correct S&OP execution and its consolidation within the company.

2

Where is S&OP used?

S&OP groups sales and supply plans and aligns all a company's areas by setting up a single transparent reality for all of them.

Its great contribution is that it provides the same data to all the company's functions so that each area can develop its own strategies, but always within a single vision of the organization's activity.

It is especially useful and very necessary in multinational groups that have several sales offices and different industrial plants or distribution centres. However, it can be applied to many types of organizations, adapting itself to each one's way of operating.

Large companies
Product-based companies
Sales and operations planning (S&OP)
SME's
Service companies

In small companies it also offers good results, since they have the same need for establishing a direct relationship between what is planned to be sold and what is planned to be made available, either from stock or by manufacturing.

Of course, it is a process that can be applied to companies from very different industries in which there are different specific needs and conditions and it is also extendable to service companies.

3

Who leads the planning process?

S&OP must be led by top management or its executive team since only then will a successful outcome be ensured.

However, S&OP must be part of the company culture and its running must be passed on to the organization as a whole.

All areas should know the significance of the conclusions derived from each meeting or report and appreciate these as a direct source of information to which they must have access.

The connection between reports from one area and another and the coherence of each one's data is the key to presenting a single truth.

Top
Management
Area 1
Area 2
Area 3
Area 4
Sales and
operations
planning
(S&OP)
Coherency
Transparency
Company
culture

Therefore, transparency must be a fundamental value of the company. There cannot be different accounting systems or different types of reports, for example.

All areas or functions should be involved in S&OP, even if they do not lead the process. Different hierarchical levels participate according to the different phases, although executive meetings require the assistance of senior management for decision making.

4

S&OP objectives

The six main objectives of the sales and operations planning process are:

1. **Creation of commercial offering with estimated delivery time**

   The sales offices inform the organization's own or third party production centres on the direction of their sales efforts and indicate which orders could be confirmed in the near future.

   In this way, the commercial offices can receive estimated production lead times from the manufacturing centres with the option of reserving the necessary capacity in them in order to negotiate with their customers and close sales.

2. Management of deviations with customers

The commercial offices can find out the status of current orders and compare their progress with initial production planning. This allows them to detect deviations in advance and be able to design alternative plans or negotiate new delivery times with customers. This can occur both in the case of potential delays to availability deadlines or conversely, when the company is interested in bringing forward some delivery in order to maintain production equilibrium.

3. Rescheduling

S&OP makes it possible to resolve conflicts and establish priorities in order to reach agreements that minimize possible damages to operations as a whole.

Rescheduling and adapting to the situation at any given time offers the option of working together on a common timeline and implementing action plans on time. For example, it may be possible to push the activity in a given moment to meet a deadline or manage potential penalties, among other options.

4. Forecasts

Both the sales offices and the manufacturing centres can prepare an activity forecast based on realistic and agreed data.

Production centres can have a clearer view of their workload and perform capacity analyses to determine labour, supplies and financing requirements.

Distribution centres or intermediate warehouses can work out how to keep the minimum stock to guarantee the agreed service rate or produce contractual security stocks when the risk of the activity requires it.

5. Strategic sales, production and financial plans

From the forecasts made by the different areas in the company, the corresponding strategic plans can be developed:

- **Sales plan.**

- **Production plan** from which the following plans are derived:

    - Supply plan – describes the purchases the company makes with respect to what it needs for its operations.

- Capacity plan – describes the utilization of available productive resources.
- Recruitment plan – to make more human resources available.
- Training plan – to train professional teams in specific areas.
- Restructuring plan – to make redundant own or external staff that are definitely not going to be needed.
- Logistics plan – to guarantee the materials supply and define how the company delivers the products its customers have bought.
- Inventory plan – makes a reasoned analysis of the stocks that will be held.

- **Financial plan** – to describe how the forecast production costs are to be borne and a sound economy maintained in the company. Two additional plans derive from it:

  - Invoicing plan – based on realistic company activity data, calendars for sales and revenue and purchases and costs can be established.
  - Treasury plan – to analyze the economic status of the company at any given moment in time.

S&OP objectives

1 Creation of commercial offering with estimated delivery time

2 Management of deviations with customers

3 Rescheduling

4 Forecasts

5 Strategic sales, production and financial plans

6 Supply Chain Strategy

6. Supply Chain Strategy

All the available information helps establish the strategy needed to fulfil commitments to customers.

Providing the most accurate demand forecasts possible is the most effective way to integrate suppliers in the supply chain.

How to develop S&OP

It is essential to appoint a process leader who will be responsible for its execution and continuous development.

This leader will call regular formal meetings between the sales and operations functions using, if possible, a pre-set schedule and requiring the compulsory attendance of senior management representing the different areas or functions so that agreements can be reached during the course of the meetings, if necessary.

It is recommended that the financial area be present, but if it cannot, it must always be provided with the outcomes agreed upon in each meeting.

It is advisable to share a pre-meeting agenda, listing the main points to be discussed. In this way, participants will be able to prepare the relevant documentation and keep up to date on the most relevant aspects to their teams in order to present or discuss their concerns in an organized way.

These meetings are not intended to surprise anyone, but rather to put all the issues and open points on the table and manage them together. An agenda also allows people who are not usually present at meetings to have the option of participating in those where there is a key discussion point that affects them or for which they are responsible.

Likewise, meeting minutes are essential. Their usefulness increases if they are circulated immediately with a summary of the conclusions and agreements reached.

Meeting minutes or additional documentation generated in the process should be distributed to all areas of the organization that may be affected by the decisions taken on issues that have been discussed and agreed upon as well as by the progress of any negotiations that are still outstanding.

During these meetings the best alternatives for the company's profitability are analysed along with the risks associated with the different situations as well as management's willingness to commit to them.

From the simulated approach to different scenarios arise the action plans as well as the contingency plans.

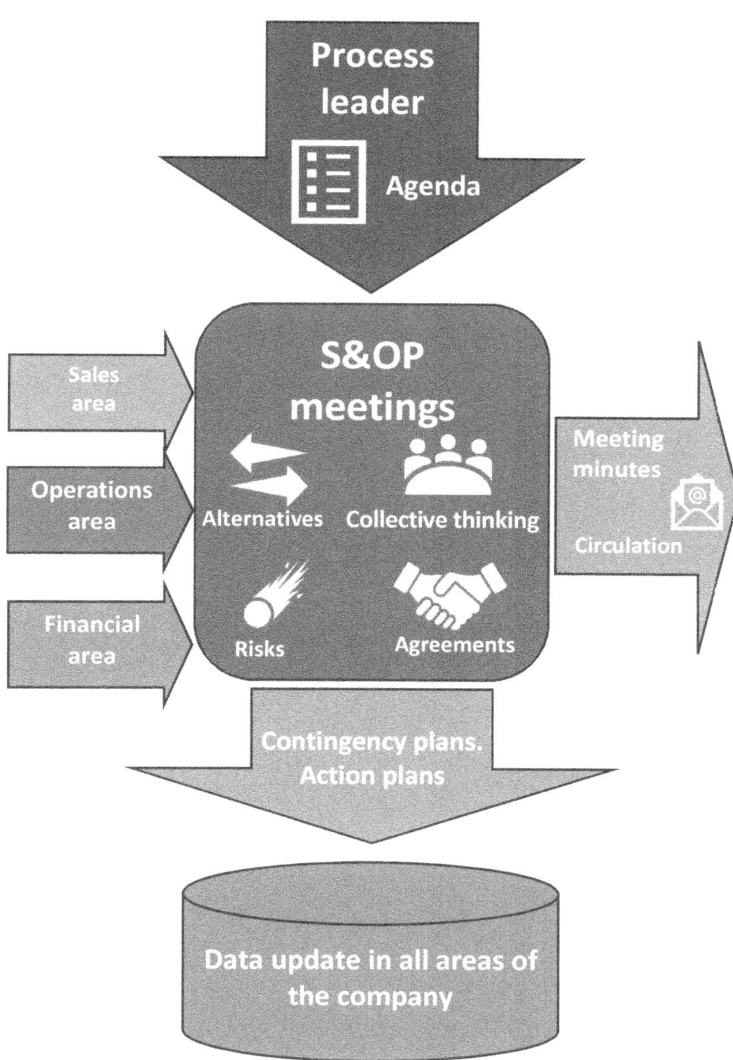

Process leader
Agenda
Sales area
Operations area
Financial area
S&OP meetings
Alternatives
Collective thinking
Risks
Agreements
Meeting minutes
Circulation
Contingency plans. Action plans
Data update in all areas of the company

This allows organizations to anticipate hypothetically adverse conditions that might occur and react proactively and systematically to them.

All areas of the company generate data which may be contained in master tables, databases or management systems and modified or updated on the basis of the reflections and agreements reached in the meetings. Subsequently, there must be a compilation process and analysis of pooled data that makes it possible to obtain a realistic situation map of the company.

6

S&OP meetings

The five main points of the sales and operations planning process that should be analyzed during the meetings are:

1. **New projects in the tender phase**

   It is good to concentrate on those with a high probability of being won as well as those that will be decided shortly.

   Moreover, it is important to analyze whether production capacity or stocks should be reserved for them. This will depend on the sales team's views and confidence in the sale being closed.

It is the sales team's responsibility to estimate the sales conversion rate of the volume in the tender phase.

2. Rescheduling during the order acquisition phase

These are projects or orders that were expected to be secured and for which, therefore, production capacity or stocks had been reserved. However, they have not yet been closed and require agile rescheduling according to the changing needs.

3. Delivery terms for secured orders

After the commercial negotiations, the secured projects or orders will have some agreed delivery terms that do not always exactly match the initial planned approach.

It is necessary to check the reserved capacity to know if it will allow delivery to be accomplished in the conditions finally committed to or if changes will have to be made.

This allows orders to be confirmed or changes in them to be requested.

It is important to determine the different stages the product will pass through – design, procurement, manufacturing, assembly, painting, quality control, etc. – in order to carry out an analysis of the potential risks that could prevent delivery to the final client from being fulfilled under the agreed conditions.

Check that it is possible to carry out the projects correctly with the information received.

Should there be any document issue or requirement that is hard to meet, now is the time to give the warning.

4. Review of work in progress

This part of the process relates to an update of the work in progress. For this, generally speaking, the following information must be provided:

- A progress report for each work in progress.
- An identification of supply chain challenges (tight deadlines, price level, supplier approval, new materials or components, regulations, etc.).

5. Analyze and discuss the availability (output) of finished product

The key question relates to the finished product availability date. This will be based on the possible stocks available in the warehouse (and therefore automatically available) or on a previous production process, depending on the production area planning.

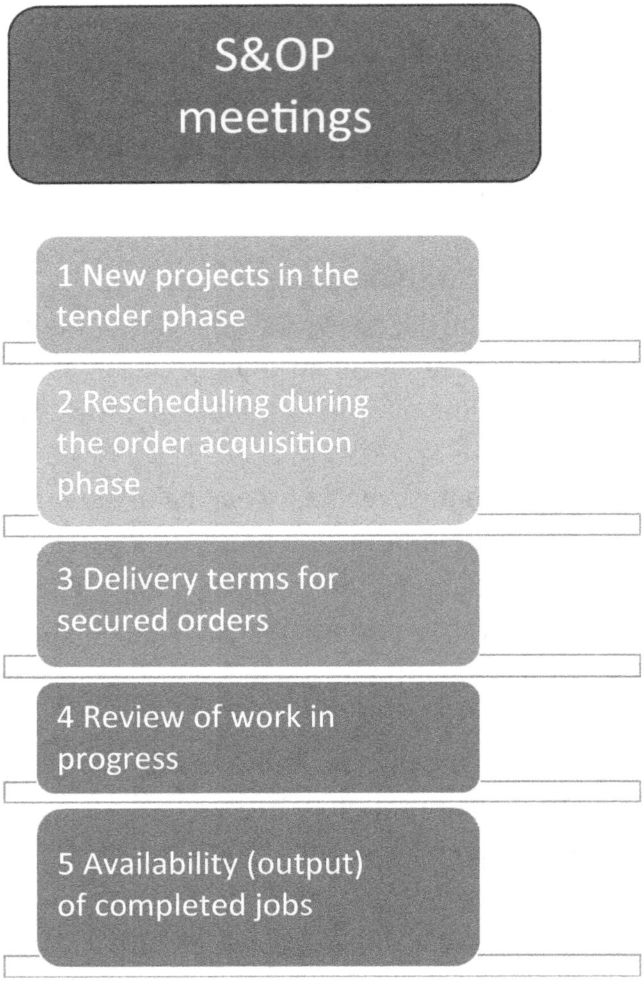

S&OP meetings

1 New projects in the tender phase

2 Rescheduling during the order acquisition phase

3 Delivery terms for secured orders

4 Review of work in progress

5 Availability (output) of completed jobs

The key points to be defined are usually:

- Loading of goods on transport unit or vehicle (who, how, when and where).
- Transport process (mode, means, price).
- Delivery terms (Incoterms rule, delivery date, customs in destination country, necessary documentation, etc.).

7

The minutes of the meetings

The minutes of the meeting contain a summary of the main issues analyzed in each meeting.

They should define the workload that is channelled from the sales area to the manufacturing or distribution areas, comparing forecast order entries with actual confirmed demand.

The minutes should also set out the total reserved capacity in the manufacturing centres and specify the projects, bids and precise work orders it corresponds to.

Another key aspect that must be defined is which priorities have been established for each work order according to customer type, penalty costs for breach of agreed conditions and other variables.

They should also reflect the fulfilment of agreed delivery dates for contracted products and the potential cost of a delay.

In addition, there are other details that should not be overlooked such as which orders are about to be secured, what characteristics the new work orders have, what types of products they are and whether there are variations or modifications planned for any work order, for example.

It is important to reflect accurately, completely and faithfully all the thoughts, potential risks discussed, participants' points of view and agreements reached.

The immediate mailing of the minutes, just after the meeting has taken place, and their immediate circulation by the different functional areas are crucial to their being a functional tool that can be counted on for later use in other areas.

A systematic layout will make the minutes easier to read and understand. It is even advisable to standardize the format with the company's management system.

To ensure the minutes are a faithful reflection of the contents of the meetings, and that the people participating in them accept them as such, the main options are:

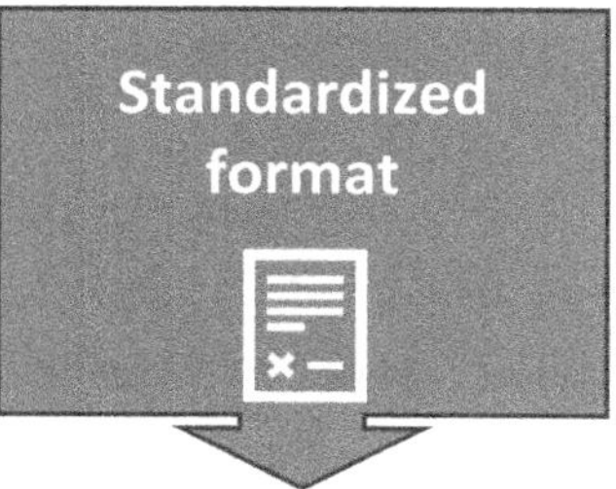

Standardized
format

Meeting minutes

• Actual confirmed demand (compared to order
estimates)
• Total reserved capacity
• Workload (from sales area to operations area)
• Work order priorities
• Agreed delivery dates (compliance review)

Thoughts, discussions, agreements

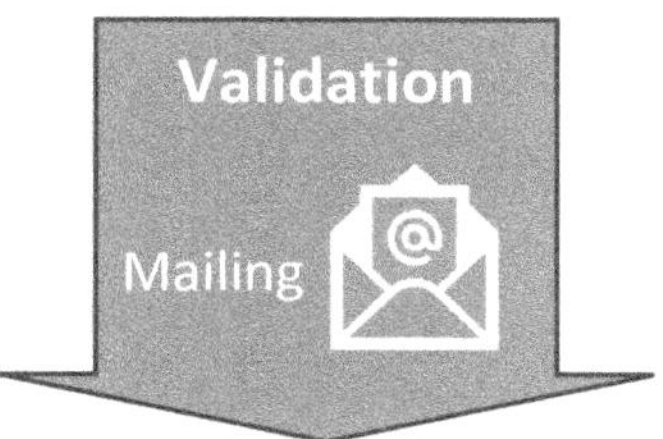

Validation

Mailing

- Anyone on the mailing list that the minutes are sent to may answer the circulated mail if he considers that something is not correct or is not accurate and requires nuance or simply if he wants to add some additional information.

- Prepare preliminary minutes to be distributed for participants' approval and, only after they all confirm should they be distributed to the rest of the organization.

- Write the minutes during the meeting itself and have it signed by all participants at the end. In videoconference meetings, the screen can be shared to write a collaborative text, allowing each written note to be agreed on in real time.

8

S&OP frequency

The product life cycle determines whether the follow-up of the sales and operations planning process is more or less frequent. The more volatile the demand and the shorter the product life cycles, the closer together the formal review periods should be.

The product life cycle largely determines the schedules, risks and costs, i.e.

- Scheduling the introduction and withdrawal of products from the market will set the planning milestones.

S&OP frequency
(Conventional approach)

S&OP meetings: monthly

Follow-up: weekly

Updates: daily

Product life cycle

S&OP follow-up with relative frequency, according to phase of product life cycle.

- The costs of each stage of the product life cycle are different as are the margins that can be obtained from them (the cost of sales in the launch and promotion stages is different from the maturity stage). It is also important to make provision for when substitutes must be found to replace the production quota kept for products that need to be withdrawn.

- Analysing the product types as a whole will make it possible to buffer against the different life cycles.

In general, executive meetings are held monthly but there should be lower-level weekly reviews as well as a daily follow-up of all incidents, planning changes, capacity changes and reports of relevant issues between areas.

9

Macro data applied to S&OP

Macro data or data intelligence, also known as big data, serve to interpret the set of data available to the company and make executive decisions based on objective criteria.

Companies with satisfactory results are distinguished precisely by their ability to interpret trends and visualize changes in time. To do this, they work by continuously interpreting the appropriate data using metrics or key indicators that measure the development of their activity and scorecards that represent their reality and offer suggestions on points for improvement and where to act.

Key indicators should be defined in a manner consistent with the objectives set by the company. For instance, the sales volume, unit price, commercial margin, stock days or service rate may be measured.

There are mathematical statistical models that collect data and organize and process them according to different parameters, thus providing an analytical image of the company – trends, critical aspects, etc.

In a nutshell, macro data provide "mathematical intelligence" to the different processes in the company. Some current models even lead to an important foundation for creativity and try to adapt to each business independently, interpreting even unstructured data that previously could not be processed.

The sales and operations planning process can benefit from the potential offered by macro data. If the company is able to extract data of sufficient quality from its operations, it can make S&OP a very efficient tool for production planning.

It will allow it to stock up, build capacity and adapt to estimated demand ahead of time and generate forecasts based less on intuition and more on figures, both for the financial areas and to optimize the supply chain.

In any case, every S&OP analysis will require common sense, business knowledge and insight, use of statistics or data management techniques and an orderly, methodical mind.

Data
(Of sufficient quality)
Macrodata
Mathematical models
Creativity and common sense
Sales and operations planning (S&OP)
Score card
Metrics (KPI)
Improvement in forecasts and decisions

The main challenges that companies face in the management of their supply chain are, precisely, demand forecasts for suppliers, bundling customer demand and logistics management.

Example

In marketing, promotions or advertising campaigns can be made based on the results of analyzing different consumer patterns.

The different customer segments are studied and a consumer profile is determined according to their shopping basket as well as their consumption habits (geographical area where they buy, types of products, average spend, shopping timetable, etc.).

Companies use these reports to correlate products that may interest one type of consumer and so offer them specific products that are more likely to sell than others. In other words, data analysis helps to perfect advertising campaigns.

10

The benefits of S&OP

There are multiple benefits for organizations that implement a sales and operations planning process. All these benefits are derived from decision-making based on verifiable data which objectively justify the decisions agreed upon.

S&OP benefits can be grouped into three sections:

1. **Five main benefits for sales offices**

    The five main benefits that sales offices or outlets receive from S&OP are:

- **Evaluation of tender deadlines**
  The sales team will need to bid and accept some delivery time requirements that, although they may seem feasible in terms of processing times, should be contrasted with the actual situation and capacity of the production centres.

  The difficulty lies in reconciling the delivery commitments demanded by customers with the best reachable dates, depending on the capacity available, or with those that could be obtained with an agreed and concrete action plan.

  There are waiting times before each process that create bottlenecks. They will not always be the same, nor will they be the same size, so the revision of partial waiting times for a specific production process will help with the realistic calculation of an up-to-date overall process time.

  Likewise, the production capacity changes and is never infinite, contrary to what computer systems sometimes presume in their configuration, so forecasts have to be compared with reality.

- **Resource reserves**
  In FI-FO (first-in / first-out) production systems, the first order to arrive is the first one handled.

The capacity reserve as well as the resource reserves and budget items are key aspects when dealing with an order committed to in tight conditions.

- **Analysis of outputs and deliveries**
  The joint review by the sales and operations areas of the order of outputs, the analysis of the origin of deviations from forecasts and the analysis of delays allow the sales team to anticipate potential problems and force action plans on a company level. This is especially important if the situation is really delicate and there are significant losses associated with it or when trying to negotiate a new delivery date with the customer.

  It also allows for creative solutions, such as relying on the use of third parties, offering additional data or flexibilities that help to simplify developments, granting prizes or greater margins to the production team that allow it to be assured of overtime, requesting urgent orders from suppliers at a higher cost or simply allowing changes in the sequence of work orders relating to an area by delaying the lead time of a customer who is less important or whose requirements are less critical in order to favour another who is in an extreme situation.

- **Client management**
  If a time commitment cannot be fulfilled, and internally no way to solve it can be found, there will be no alternative but to go to the end customer and explain the situation.

  Knowing how to manage nonconformities with customers is an art and their satisfaction or dissatisfaction with the company often depends on it.

  Non-compliance puts the costs associated with unfulfilment, the company's brand image and the customer's future relationship with it at stake.

  That is why it is important to act as soon as possible – communicate any non-recoverable delay to the customer as soon as it is known and have a positive communication flow, including proofs and evidence of progress when monitoring might be relevant and penalties at stake.

- **Sales plan**
  The sales area, based on the demand it has assessed and knowing what the agreed capacity can allow it, will establish its priorities and establish its sales plan.

Supply analysis
Resource reserves
Output analysis
Customer management
Sales plan

2. Five main benefits for production centres

The five main benefits that production and distribution centres receive from S&OP are:

- **Work forecast based on actual sales prospects**

  This means producing according to what the commercial function, close to the customer and the market, estimates in a sales plan and not according to the intuitions that the production area might consider.

- **Evaluate own capacity**

  The capacity of facilities, equipment, machinery and labour is evaluated well in advance to determine whether or not the estimated workload is feasible and whether or not the available capacity could satisfy requirements.

  With sufficient foresight and time, capacity can be modified by the expansion or reduction of productive or warehousing spaces via purchase or rental operations. It is also possible to make adaptations to machinery, tools and other equipment.

  Regarding human resources, it is possible to expand or reduce the available labour force as well as subcontract or outsource areas where a heavy workload is foreseen.

Another aspect to be considered is that of training staff well in advance, either because they are new hires or because their versatility and adaptation to new functions is sought.

Finally, it is possible to establish flexible work schedules, adapted to seasonality, or specific holiday shifts that allow operations to continue in each area.

- **Supply chain analysis**
  Supply chain analysis makes it easier to collaborate more closely with suppliers and negotiate deadlines, quantities or service rates ahead of time; involving them in the order volume forecasts and possible delivery deadlines necessary to meet estimated demand.

  It is possible to know which rebate or potential discount on list price suppliers can offer according to consumption volumes.

  It also encourages the search for new materials or new suppliers if current ones are at risk of not having sufficient capacity and initiating new evaluation and approval processes ahead of time.

- **Prioritization of dates**

  The planning of the work orders for the different orders entails classifying them by order of entry.

  Regardless of the action plans that can be developed in the course of an activity to streamline the various processes that comprise it (design, procurement, manufacturing, assembly, etc.), initial planning always marks the sequence in which each order is entered in the cycle and determines the overall result of the production process.

  Obviously, it is planned and rescheduled throughout the entire activity and it is crucial to know why and on what basis these actions are being done. Sometimes it is for productivity and efficiency reasons, to take advantage of batches, moulds, running machines, etc. In other cases, planning changes respond to customer wishes, which should be given higher or lower priority according to their order volumes and importance to the company's profit and loss account.

  But there will be times when the initial planning will have to be modified due to requirements that involve a penalty surcharge if certain requirements are not met, such as:

- Contractual agreements.
- Commitments related to the installation phase (e.g. machinery and auxiliary equipment that are essential for the job and will only be available for a specified period of time).
- Documentary credits.

In these cases, dialogue between all parties, under the supervision and final decision of their senior managements, is what will define the correct prioritization that best benefits the company as a whole.

- **Production plan**
  The production area, on the basis of estimated demand and after considering whether or not to adapt capacity, will establish the volume that can be served, schedule it according to agreed priorities and establish its production plan.

SALES AND OPERATIONS PLANNING S&OP IN 14 STEPS

3. **The five main benefits for the company or the business group**

The five major benefits companies and business groups receive from S&OP are:

- **Activity forecast based on realistic sales estimates**
  Estimated demand is calculated with real time data based on the status of the sales area's business dealings.

- **Invoicing Plan**
  Based on estimated activity and availability deadlines, an invoicing schedule can be established with the corresponding amounts. This is known as the invoicing plan.

- **Treasury plan**
  In accordance with the estimated billing and according to each project's sales terms, a receivables schedule can be established, commonly called a treasury plan.

- **Customer management and resource analysis**
  The management of the company obtains unique knowledge of:

  - The evolution of sales by geographical areas, customer segments and product type.
  - The potential market.
  - The conversion rate of sales leads to orders.
  - The status of each order.
  - The production capacity and restrictions on same; the resources deployed to modify it.
  - The delays and their impact on billing and treasury.
  - The investments that must be made to meet the sales targets.
  - Conflicts with customers.
  - Supply chain issues.

- **General estimates**
  Top management will be able to establish sound general estimates based on reconciled data.

> The key advantage of S&OP is the integration of high-level strategic plans with day-to-day operations.

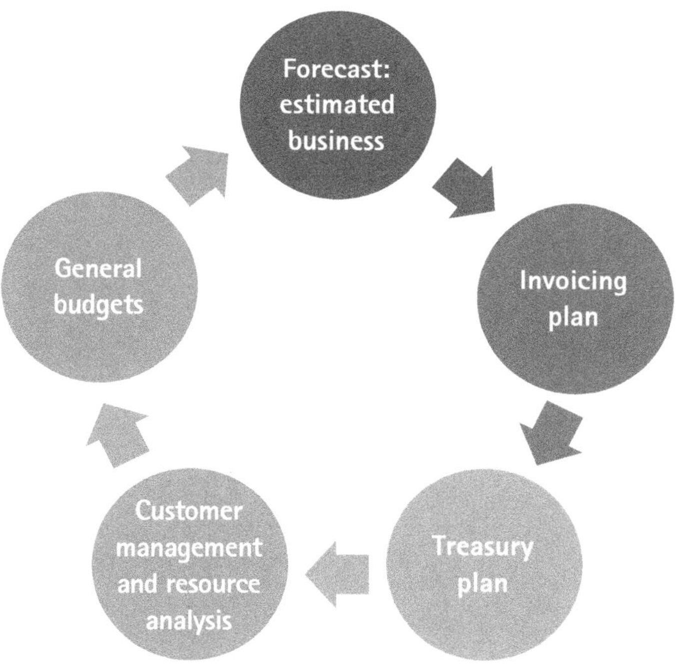

Forecast: estimated business
Invoicing plan
Treasury plan
Customer management and resource analysis
General budgets

11

S&OP as a process

S&OP is a process that must have inputs, outputs, necessary resources (records and associated documentation) and control mechanisms (indicators).

It may appear with its completed process sheet in an ISO 9001 management system, identifying the following five sections:

1. Inputs

- **Sales area information** (unsecured orders, confirmed orders, customer expectations and priorities)

- **Delivery area information:**
  - Purchases: estimated delivery times, possible discounts depending on consumption, suppliers' working conditions, etc.
  - Production: estimated workload, utilization level of productive capacity, production planning, estimated processing times, resource requirements, status of work in progress and finished products in warehouse.

- **Finance area information:** state of company cash flow, financing needs, scheduled payments and billing deadlines, among others.

2. **Outputs**
   - Balance between demand and supply (production and purchases).
   - Aggregate sales and operations plan.
   - Financial plan.
   - Optimized supply chain.
   - Unique and transparent information.
   - Holistic vision of the company.

3. **Resources**
   - Data processing.
   - Data analysis.
   - Status reports.

- Planning meetings.
- Communication systems (when participants in S&OP meetings are in different geographic locations).

4. Control mechanisms

- Accuracy of data input in process.
- Quality of processing and analysis of the necessary data.
- Level of compliance of planned schedules.
- Percentage of conflicts resolved satisfactorily.
- Level of availability of resources required for the process.
- Accuracy and diffusion of meeting minutes.

To fulfil an ISO 9001 management system, a sales and operations planning process involves a whole range of associated documentation. The most significant documents are:

- Inventory.
- Activity forecast.
- Sales plan.
- Capacity plan.
- Supply plan.
- Invoicing plan.
- Treasury plan.
- General budgets.

In addition, the operation of the process must be recorded in a set of records, the main ones being:

- Agendas.
- Meeting minutes.
- Consolidated plans.

On the other hand, it must be taken into account that the document describing the process will have to define the following five points:

- **S&OP aim**
  Formalize a demand and delivery review between sales offices and production centres in a regular, structured manner and focus attention on the amount of present and future orders.

- **S&OP scope**
  This includes the executive S&OP in terms of analysis and decision making process. It does not include production planning or the daily activity schedule.

- **S&OP owner**
  The manager assigned to lead S&OP.

- **S&OP participants**
  The people responsible for the sales, operations and finance areas and the managing director of the company (CEO).

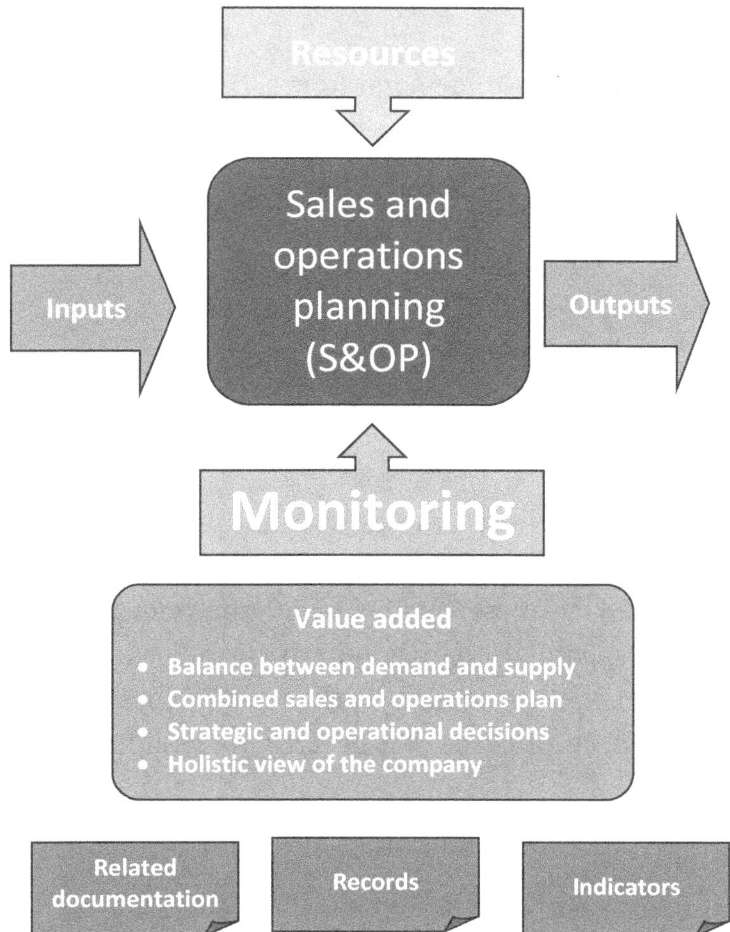

Resources
Inputs
Sales and operations planning (S&OP)
Outputs
Monitoring
Value added
• Balance between demand and supply
• Combined sales and operations plan
• Strategic and operational decisions
• Holistic view of the company
Related documentation
Records
Indicators

- **S&OP indicators**
  Those management indicators that must be moni-
  tored on a dashboard and which indicate the performance level of the process, for example:

  - Accuracy of demand forecast.
  - Availability of the scheduled resources.
  - Service level.
  - Deliveries made on time.
  - Inventory level.
  - Utilization of production capacity.
  - Transport cost on sales.
  - Variations on production plan.
  - Non-conformities with customers.

The result of the process will be to match demand
and supply, reflected in an aggregate plan that will be
integrated in a master table (originating from a spread-
sheet file, database or computer management system)
as well as the agreements reached and discussions held
that were recorded in the different meeting minutes.

Identification of bottlenecks

Identifying the bottlenecks in a process makes the day-to-day restrictions on fulfilling the company objectives more visible.

In his novel *The Goal*, Eliyahu M. Goldratt established the well-known Theory of Constraints that shows the existence of limitations derived from physical processes, the market or the company's own culture which must be managed in order to optimize production and match it to demand.

An appropriate forecast of the constraints helps to visualize different future scenarios and evaluate how to adapt the company in order to better position it against foreseeable future circumstances (projected workload, customer expectations, market context, etc.).

Linear prediction models for demand based on historical data only take into account the rising or falling demand trend in the analyzed period of time and become misaligned and produce major errors due to market fluctuations.

These are optimistic models for predicting positive results in periods of rising demand. They work very well to detect the need to expand the workforce, create a larger productive area, increase available inventory and offer high expectations in order to seek funding. However, these models react late and adjust poorly when demand volatility exists.

In addition, there may also be other constraints (limitations on production capacity, minimum manufacturing quantities, maximum warehousing capacity, customer delivery schedule, etc.) that may make the delivery plan fail to meet estimated demand.

A sales and operations planning process that shares and jointly analyzes information from the sales, production and financial areas highlights the real constraints that must be managed.

In short, S&OP seeks to soften the effect of fluctuations in market demand as well as the effects of other bottlenecks that may exist in the organization and it acts as a catalyst to prevent sudden changes from impacting the profit and loss account and to achieve a final balance between sales and operations.

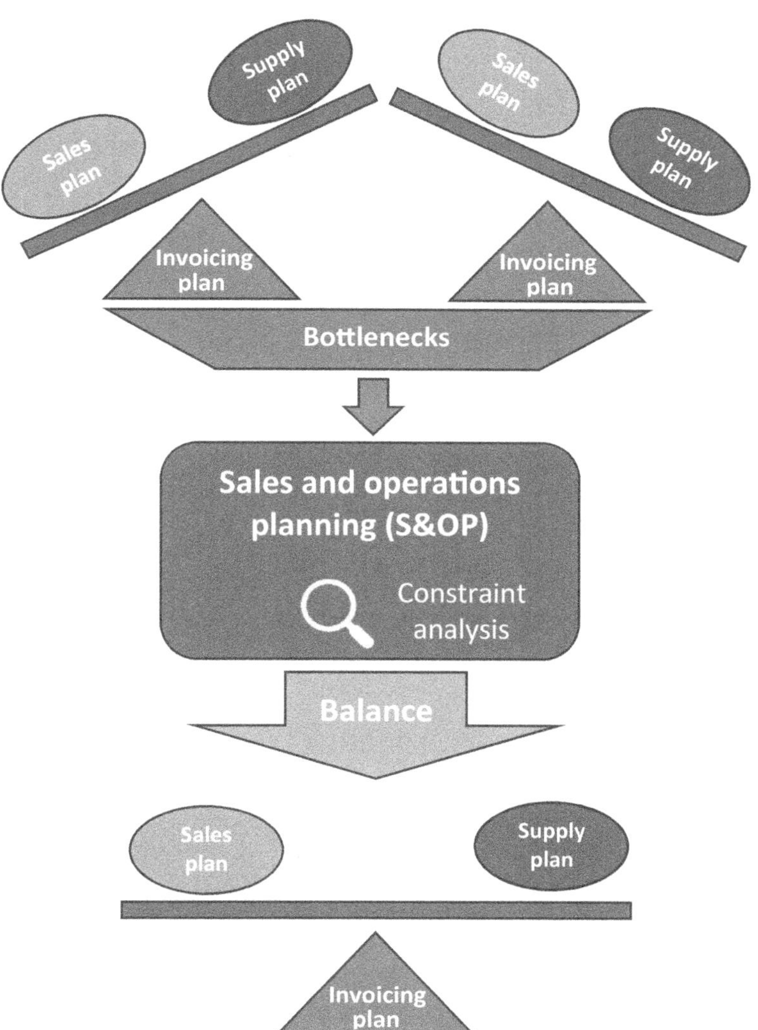

Supply plan
Sales plan
Sales plan
Supply plan
Invoicing plan
Invoicing plan
Bottlenecks
Sales and operations planning (S&OP)
Constraint analysis
Balance
Sales plan
Supply plan
Invoicing plan

13

General budgets

A great benefit of a sales and operations planning process is that it helps develop companies' general budgets.

S&OP is an aggregate plan that gives a global vision but originates from highly detailed information. Each productive capacity is reserved for a specific job, although it is the sum total of the order book that provides the information used to take strategic decisions such as an enlargement or reduction of the workforce or the acquisition of new machinery or new workspaces. In this way, it provides data to make a sound judgement before assuming certain expenses and investments.

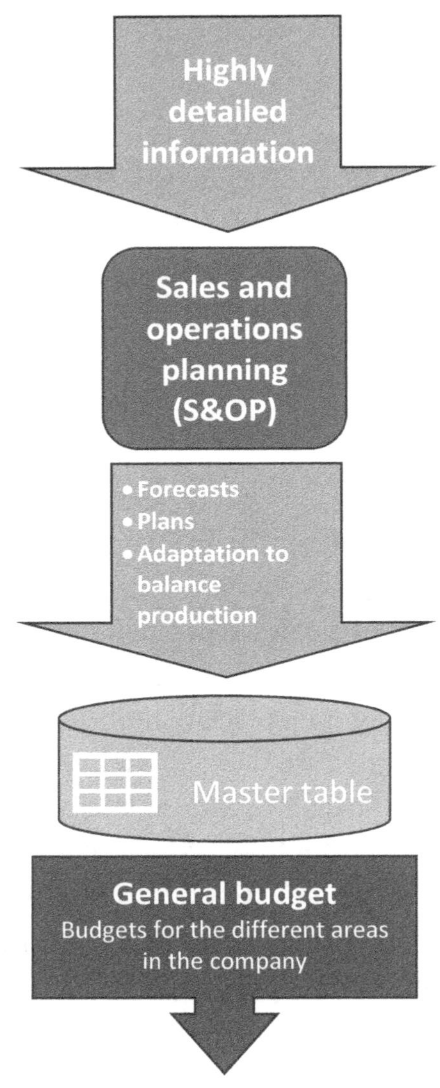

Highly detailed information
Sales and operations planning (S&OP)
• Forecasts
• Plans
• Adaptation to balance production
Master table
General budget
Budgets for the different areas in the company

S&OP makes it possible to know simultaneously the sales volume, margin, labour and related material costs according to the demand forecast for the coming year. With this data, it is possible to establish budgets for the different areas.

In other words, knowing what is going to be sold and at what profit, it is possible to calculate what is going to be invoiced and when it will be paid. Likewise, the staff and related resources required to meet the expected demand are known so that the costs of personnel and the material to be procured to carry out the necessary jobs can be calculated. Based on the final balance obtained, strategic decisions such as an expansion of the business or the development of new products can be taken.

Using a master table or computer system that relates everything, all the key values will be available – value of the work orders, arrival date of the materials in the production centre, issue date of finished products, invoicing and payment dates, etc. – all of which are milestones in the preparation of the general budgets.

14

Forecasts and plans

A sales and operations planning process makes it possible to forecast the volume and type of materials required. From this forecast a purchasing plan that will help in negotiating with suppliers can be generated.

It is also possible to manage the distribution logistics process and plan freight shipments, ensuring the availability and coordination of the necessary means of transport are located in the right place and at the right time for loading and distributing on time and within the stipulated costs.

In the same way, a production plan can be made, stocks can be managed and the availability of warehousing planned.

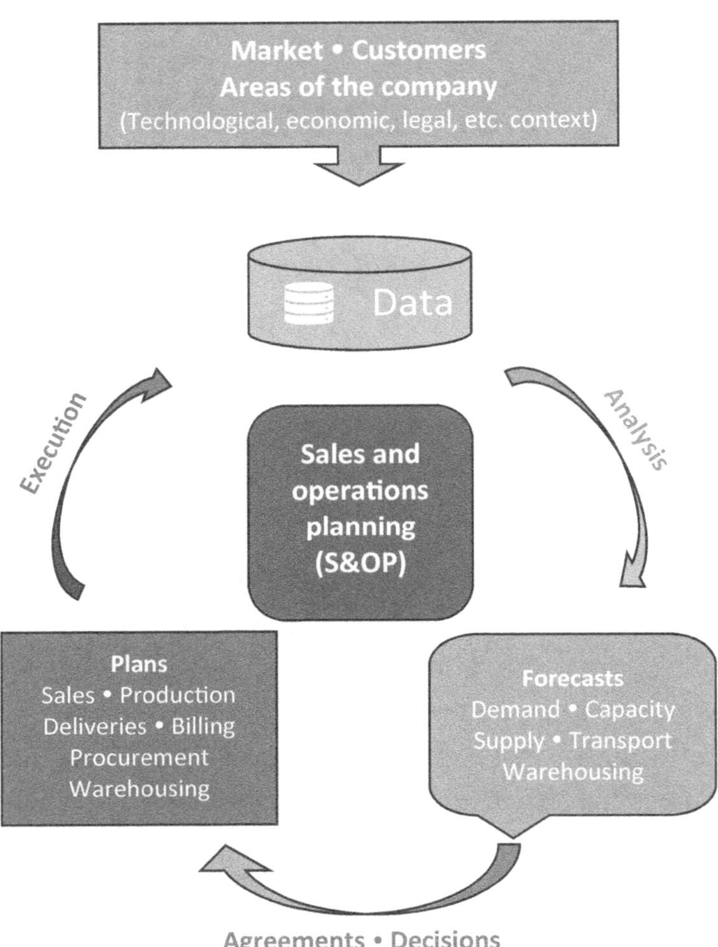

Market • Customers
Areas of the company
(Technological, economic, legal, etc. context)
Data
Execution
Analysis
Sales and operations planning (S&OP)
Plans
Sales • Production
Deliveries • Billing
Procurement
Warehousing
Forecasts
Demand • Capacity
Supply • Transport
Warehousing
Agreements • Decisions

In addition to developing these plans, activity forecasts can be made and general budgets adjusted to a more realistic estimate as the activity takes place and the actual figures are consolidated. In that case, S&OP allows us to analyze what factors have led to variations in the margin – volume, product type, price or cost, for example.

That means, in general terms, it is possible to anticipate any deterioration in the company's performance level and react in a timely manner.

S&OP is, therefore, a process founded on planning based on data analysis and rescheduling in order to adapt operations to circumstances at any given moment but especially on fluent communication and transparency when it comes to spreading key information.

In conclusion, by means of a sales and operations planning process, the company produces a single truth from the top down.

Case studies

The person in charge of logistics in a pharmaceutical company applies the manufacturing plan as an entry in their shipping process.

This production plan is modified frequently according to the constraints that the supply chain generates when certain elements are received late or when there are problems in the production process itself such as machinery breakdowns or resultant non-conforming medicines that are rejected by control techniques.

The delays in the production process give rise to a rescheduling that the production area carries out according to its own criteria.

At one stage, the logistics area detects that lately the same customer is on the receiving end of order backlogs. All this customer's orders are suffering a poor service rate following delays in all their deliveries.

Concerned about customer satisfaction, the person in charge of the logistics area speaks to the head of the production area. It seems that priority is systematically being given to certain orders for a key customer, meaning that similar orders for other customers are bumped down the queue, thereby lengthening the lead time.

The logistics area cannot determine for itself whether the key customer being favoured is more important or not than the one being harmed, although the number of delayed consignments and the delay per consignment seem excessive.

This is a recurring situation in many companies. Bottlenecks tend to be solved by hurting a customer or certain orders without making a real analysis of the situation.

S&OP makes it possible to jointly analyze the conflicting situations between requirements and deliveries with all areas in the company.

Under S&OP, the problem of capacity or delay in the delivery of materials would have been discussed, the suppliable demand would have been estimated and some jobs would have been prioritized over others, according to their contribution to company profits, the opportunity cost and the criticality of the situation to

Without S&OP

- The causes of bottlenecks are not properly analyzed.

- The production area modifies the production plan without considering other criteria.

- A customer who may be strategically important is harmed.

Under S&OP

- Bottlenecks are analyzed and the restrictions that provoke them are detected.

- The production plan is modified by consensus.

- The possible consequences of each rescheduling are evaluated.

the client and the consequential commercial damage that would occur.

Perhaps the disadvantaged client was a strategic piece for the positioning of the company in a particular country and it would have been preferable not to offer them poor service. Maybe one of said client's batches could have borne a delay but not others. If they had been consulted by the sales team and offered transparent information, the client would have been able to understand the situation and actively contribute to improving the results.

A company's general budget is made by taking the previous year's as a benchmark. Growth of 3% is estimated since that is what the country estimates for the gross domestic product (GDP). Accordingly, the workforce is kept on and, in addition, some land is bought because the price is right.

Suddenly, the industry slumps due to the emergence of new technologies that lead to the appearance of alternative products that were previously unfeasible. On top of this, the country is in the early stages of a recession that has not yet been analyzed to correct the GDP growth forecast. The result is a 30% reduction in company revenues.

Without S&OP

- Information in all areas of the company is not analyzed before making decisions.

- Planning is based on unreliable predictions.

- The financial area is not aware of some decisions or planning.

Under S&OP

- Data from all areas of the company are jointly analyzed.

- Forecasts are made and planning is done according to them.

- The financial area has full knowledge of all company planning.

The situation is one of total emergency.

Under S&OP, the sales team would have warned top management about the lack of orders or growth expectations for the following year, as well as some negative changes already detected in the market. Accordingly, the workforce would have been cut back, no investments would have been made and a more in-depth analysis would have been made of the scenario that might occur in the immediate future.

Case study

3

The general manager of a company that manufactures industrial refrigeration machinery, with a wide offering of different ranges and sizes, pays its sales team a variable salary according to the monthly turnover they have contributed to the company.

This company is national leader in sophisticated machinery, especially in the development of tailor-made projects. However, in smaller machinery it competes with a large number of small manufacturers and loses significant market share.

The sales director of the central region is the one that contributes 65% of total turnover as it is entitled to bid for business with the large national companies but it is focusing all its efforts on selling large machines because they are the ones that produce the highest turnover.

At a certain point, the production manager talks to the management of the company to let them know that the assembly staff on the production lines of the smaller machines is at a standstill. In fact, while the large machinery production lines are causing a bottleneck in the delivery of finished product, other staff have no workload and cannot perform any other tasks because they are not trained for them and cannot operate machines whose complexity is beyond their knowledge.

In the implementation of a sales and operations planning process, during the capacity evaluation and adaptation of the workload in the different production lines, the process itself would have indicated the need to receive more orders for the range of small machinery.

After an analysis of why the sales of these products had fallen, it would have been detected that these ranges were not being offered because the sales team tends to work hardest on what produces the highest turnover and, consequently, the highest bonuses and salary.

So, based on that initial analysis, the conditions would have been there to:

Without S&OP

- There is an incomplete picture of the company's situation.
- Workload is not estimated based on real data.
- Strategic plans are designed without taking into account information from all areas.

Under S&OP

- The workload and available capacity level are evaluated and trends and constraints are analyzed.
- The reality of the company and the causes of deviations are known.
- Rescheduling is done so that the company can adapt to circumstances at any given moment.

- Realign the company's own objectives with those of the management team and the rest of the personnel. As long as the organization is interested in sustaining all the current lines of work, it will be understood that it is necessary to reward the sales people for achieving turnover objectives in each one of the product ranges rather than overall turnover.

- Going forward, if it is considered that the company is not competitive in the small machinery range due to the high number of competitors and that, even though the sales team is rewarded, orders are not obtained except when profitability is greatly reduced, that range could be left as a residual product and the associated personnel trained to make them interchangeable with those of the large machinery range.

Case study

4

A Japanese manufacturer of electrical equipment has a distribution warehouse in the outskirts of a large city. One of the advantages they offer is their excellent delivery time in the whole central area – any reference within 24-48 hours – for which they have guaranteed stocks to ensure continuous supply.

The consumption trend of recent months has been rising and the factory has sent high levels of stock from Japan so that the service rate does not fail.

Several customers have suspended their distribution contract with the company in the past month due to the recent increase in price lists sent by the sales department.

Without S&OP

- Demand is estimated using linear models which only take into account the historical trend and not possible market fluctuations and changes.

- Changes are made without analyzing possible consequences such as rising prices.

Under S&OP

- The supply plan is designed according to forecasts worked out between all areas of the company.

- Market trends are analyzed in detail.

- The effect of changes is reviewed and rescheduling is done when necessary.

At the end of the year, the inventory shows alarming figures and the plant in Japan does not understand how a distribution centre could hold such a volume of assets without releasing it.

Under a sales and operations planning process, the replenishment of new material would not have been estimated according to the delivery history and past trends but rather on future forecasts discussed with the sales team. The sales team would have commented on their expectations for lower sales throughout the year due to the new price lists and the refusal of many customers to accept them.

That way, they would have determined the ideal stock required for the new potential market and to guarantee satisfactory delivery. Also, if the commercial impact of the new prices proves to be greater than estimated, exceptions could be made in the prices of certain orders to release the material and thereby avoid a large inventory and its obsolescence.

Case study

5

An SME has a sales person whose objective is to sell what the factory says it will finish producing the following week. For this reason, the sales person uses the necessary discount to sell the goods being produced to a customer, thereby avoiding warehousing as they have hardly any space for this purpose.

Every time a sale is forced, margins are reduced so much that the company is currently running at a loss.

With S&OP, the margins of the products that are sold would have been analyzed by the different areas to see how the volume of the combined set of products affects the overall margins and operating profit. In this

Without S&OP

- The sales plan and the production plan are not reconciled profitably for the company.

- There is no overall view of the company so no problem situations are detected.

- Profitability is not maximized.

Under S&OP

- Strategies based on analysis of realistic and complete information are presented.

- Production is optimized, based on sales forecasts derived from the commercial area's information.

way, different sales strategies could have been devised to avoid eroding the company's profitability. Thus, it could have opted for actions such as the following:

- Do not sell rather than doing so at an excessively low price or do not manufacture, despite the cost of having workers and machinery at a standstill. A relevant factor in this case is the cost of materials versus the hours of work involved.
- Store products rather than selling below cost if it is anticipated that they can be sold at a higher margin within a reasonable period of time.
- Commercial support from the company management.
- Round out the products with additional features such as extensions of guarantees and after-sales services, etc., which do not necessarily imply a reduction of the commercial margin.

Collection: Gestiona
Publishing director: David Soler

Sales and operations planning. S&OP in 14 steps
1st edition, 2017
© Cristina Peña Andrés
© of this edition including cover design: ICG Marge, SL
© cover photograph: Shutterstock, r.classen

Publisher: Marge Books
València, 558 - 08026 Barcelona
Tel. 931 429 486 - marge@margebooks.com
www.margebooks.com

Managing editor: Hèctor Soler
Translator: Henry O'Donnell
Infographics: Alberto Tundidor
Mark-up editor: Mercedes Lara
Printed by: Book Print Digital, SA (L'Hospitalet de Llobregat, Barcelona)

ISBN: 978-84-17313-00-5
Legal Deposit: B 25858-2017

The paper used in this book has not been bleached with elemental chlorine (Cl_2).

Cómo hacer de la cadena de suministro un centro de valor
Angel Caja Corral

Cadena de suministro 4.0.
Alberto Tundidor, Eva Hernández, Cristina Peña, Javier Martínez, Javier Campos, Carlos Hernández

El crédito documentario y el mensaje SWIFT
Luis Sánchez Cañizares

La investigación en seguridad. Del Titanic a la ingeniería de la resiliencia
Jaime Rodrigo de Larrucea

Manual del comercio electrónico
Eva María Hernández Ramos, Luis Carlos Hernández Barrueco

Sales and operations planning. S&OP in 14 steps
Cristina Peña Andrés

Economías transformadoras de Barcelona
Ruben Suriñach Padilla

Planificación de ventas y operaciones. S&OP en 14 claves
Cristina Peña Andrés

Cómo participar en ferias comerciales
Cristina Peña Andrés

Manual de prevención de riesgos laborales
Blas Gómez

La economia social y solidaria en Barcelona
Ivan Miró, Anna Fernàndez

Negociación para el comercio internacional
Cristina Peña Andrés

Manual del manipulador de alimentos
Blas Gómez

La economía social y solidaria en Barcelona
Anna Fernàndez, Ivan Miró

Manual de seguridad en el trabajo
Marge Books

Cómo innovar en las pymes. Manual de mejora a través de la innovación
Alberto Tundidor Díaz

Guía documental para exportar e importar. Los 12 documentos clave
Alberto García Trius

Mass customization. Las claves de la personalización masiva
Blas Gómez Gómez

Crédito documentario. Guía para el éxito en su gestión
Cristina Peña Andrés, Amelia de Andrés Leal

Guía práctica de las reglas Incoterms® 2010
David Soler

Certificación Lean Six Sigma Green Belt para la excelencia en los negocios
Lean Six Sigma Institute, SC

Certificación Lean Six Sigma Yellow Belt para la excelencia en los negocios
Lean Six Sigma Institute, SC

Negociación intercultural. Estrategias y técnicas de negociación internacional
Domingo Cabeza, Pelayo Corella, Carlos Jiménez

Las reglas Incoterms® 2010. Manual para usarlas con eficacia
Alfonso Cabrera Cánovas

Regímenes aduaneros económicos y procesos logísticos en el comercio internacional
Pedro Coll

Inglés náutico normalizado para las comunicaciones marítimas
José Manuel Díaz Pérez

Shipping & Commercial Case Law
Albert Badia

Gestión medioambiental en la industria
José M.ª Suris

Gestión financiera del comercio internacional
Josep M.ª Casadejús

Manual de gestión aduanera. Normativas del comercio internacional y modelos de integración económica
Pedro Coll

Los abordajes en la mar
Carlos F. Salinas

El desorden sanitario tiene cura. Desde la seguridad del paciente hasta la sostenibilidad del sistema sanitario con la gestión por procesos
Rajaram Govindarajan

Gestión y liderazgo en una empresa de seguros
Simón Mahfoud y Digna Peña